U.S.A. TRAVEL GUIDES

ARKANSAS

BY ANN HEINRICHS · ILLUSTRATED BY MATT KANIA

Published by The Child's World®
1980 Lookout Drive • Mankato, MN 56003-1705
800-599-READ • www.childsworld.com

Photo Credits

Photographs ©: Shutterstock Images, cover, 1, 38 (bottom); OakleyOriginals CC2.0, 7; Rennett Stowe CC2.0, 8; Garry Tucker/USFWS, 11; Conway Area Chamber of Commerce, 12; Joe Arrigo/Shutterstock Images, 15; Zach Frank/Shutterstock Images, 16; Arkansas Department of Parks and Tourism, 19; Adam Bartlett CC2.0, 20; Bonita R. Cheshier/Shutterstock Images, 23; Jo Naylor CC2.0, 24; Josh Grenier CC2.0, 27; Stuart Seeger CC2.0, 28; Denis and Yulia Pogostins/Shutterstock Images, 31; Jeff Noble CC2.0, 32; Bryan Kemp CC2.0, 35; Rest Image/Shutterstock Images, 38 (top)

ISBN 9781503819443
LCCN 2016961121

Printing

Printed in the United States of America
PA02334

Ann Heinrichs is the author of more than 100 books for children and young adults. She has also enjoyed successful careers as a children's book editor and an advertising copywriter. Ann grew up in Fort Smith, Arkansas, and lives in Chicago, Illinois.

About the Author
Ann Heinrichs

Matt Kania loves maps and, as a kid, dreamed of making them. In school he studied geography and cartography, and today he makes maps for a living. Matt's favorite thing about drawing maps is learning about the places they represent. Many of the maps he has created can be found in books, magazines, videos, Web sites, and public places.

About the
Map Illustrator
Matt Kania

On the cover: Lawmakers meet at the Arkansas state capitol.

OUR ARKANSAS TRIP

ARKANSAS

What shall we do in Arkansas today? It's a great place to explore! Just look what's waiting down the road.

You'll roam through forests full of wildlife. You'll take a wild canoe ride. You'll soak in piping hot water. You'll dig for diamonds you can keep. You'll get a toad and watch it race. And you'll stuff yourself with tomatoes!

There's much more to do here. So we'd better get started! Just buckle up and hang on tight. We're off to discover Arkansas!

WELCOME TO
ARKANSAS

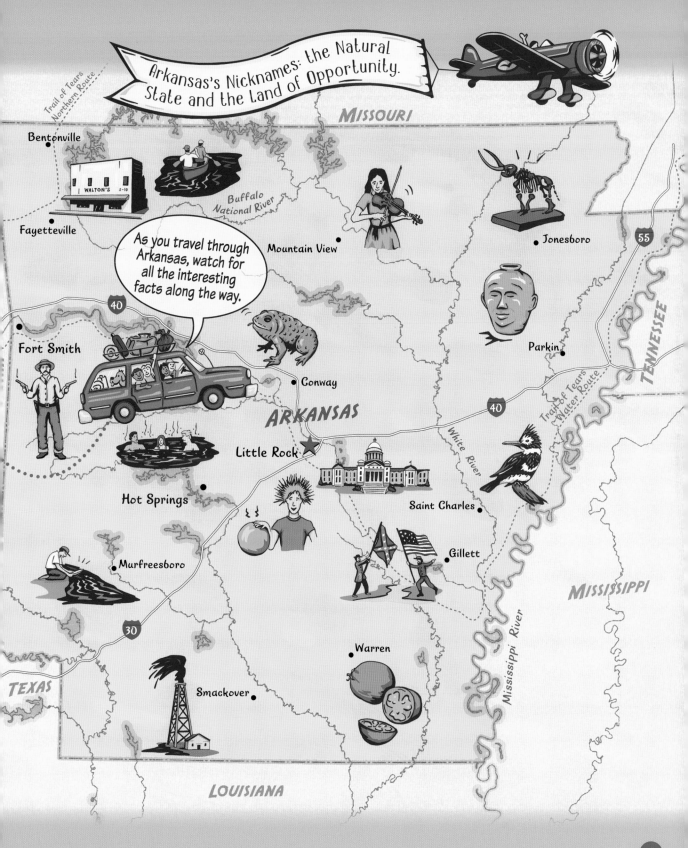

Arkansas's Nicknames: the Natural State and the Land of Opportunity.

Trail of Tears Northern Route

MISSOURI

Bentonville

WALTON'S 5-10

Fayetteville

Buffalo National River

Mountain View

Jonesboro

55

TENNESSEE

Parkin

As you travel through Arkansas, watch for all the interesting facts along the way.

40

Fort Smith

Conway

ARKANSAS

40

White River

Trail of Tears Water Route

Little Rock

Hot Springs

Saint Charles

Gillett

MISSISSIPPI

Murfreesboro

Warren

30

Mississippi River

TEXAS

Smackover

LOUISIANA

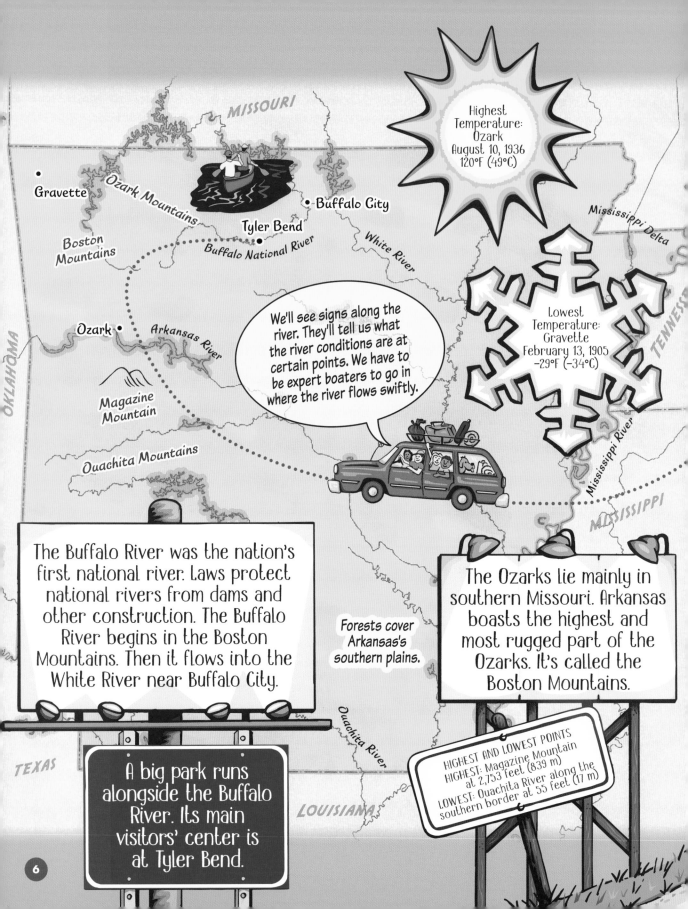

MISSISSIPPI

MISSOURI

Gravette

Ozark Mountains

Buffalo City

Tyler Bend

Boston Mountains

Buffalo National River

White River

Ozark

Arkansas River

Magazine Mountain

Ouachita Mountains

OKLAHOMA

Mississippi Delta

Mississippi River

TENNESSEE

MISSISSIPPI

Highest Temperature: Ozark August 10, 1936 120°F (49°C)

Lowest Temperature: Gravette February 13, 1905 −29°F (−34°C)

We'll see signs along the river. They'll tell us what the river conditions are at certain points. We have to be expert boaters to go in where the river flows swiftly.

The Buffalo River was the nation's first national river. Laws protect national rivers from dams and other construction. The Buffalo River begins in the Boston Mountains. Then it flows into the White River near Buffalo City.

Forests cover Arkansas's southern plains.

The Ozarks lie mainly in southern Missouri. Arkansas boasts the highest and most rugged part of the Ozarks. It's called the Boston Mountains.

Ouachita River

TEXAS

LOUISIANA

A big park runs alongside the Buffalo River. Its main visitors' center is at Tyler Bend.

HIGHEST AND LOWEST POINTS
HIGHEST: Magazine Mountain at 2,753 feet (839 m)
LOWEST: Ouachita River along the southern border at 55 feet (17 m)

CANOEING THE BUFFALO NATIONAL RIVER

Wahoo! What a wild ride! You'll love canoeing down the Buffalo National River. Some sections are smooth, but some are rough. Hang on tight!

This river winds through the Ozark Mountains. The Ozarks cover north and northwest Arkansas. They slope down toward the Arkansas River. This river flows southeast across the state. It empties into the great Mississippi River. The Ouachita Mountains reach into west-central Arkansas. Many lakes and streams sparkle among the mountains. Hot-water springs bubble up from underground, too. The Mississippi River forms Arkansas's eastern border. Land along the river is very fertile. It's often called the Mississippi Delta.

Canoe down the Buffalo National River. If you need a break, take a dip in the cool water!

IN HOT WATER IN HOT SPRINGS

Suppose you say you're in hot water. What does that mean?

It means you're in big trouble! But not in Hot Springs. Here, it means you're taking a healthful bath!

Hot springs is a national park. The water gushes from 47 underground springs. It is pumped into buildings along **Bathhouse** Row.

Try a nice, hot soak. But there's much more to do around here. Hot Springs National Park covers a big area. Hike through its forested mountains. Just don't get too close to a steep mountainside. You'll be in hot water!

Lamar Bathhouse is one of eight old bathhouses that you can find in Hot Springs.

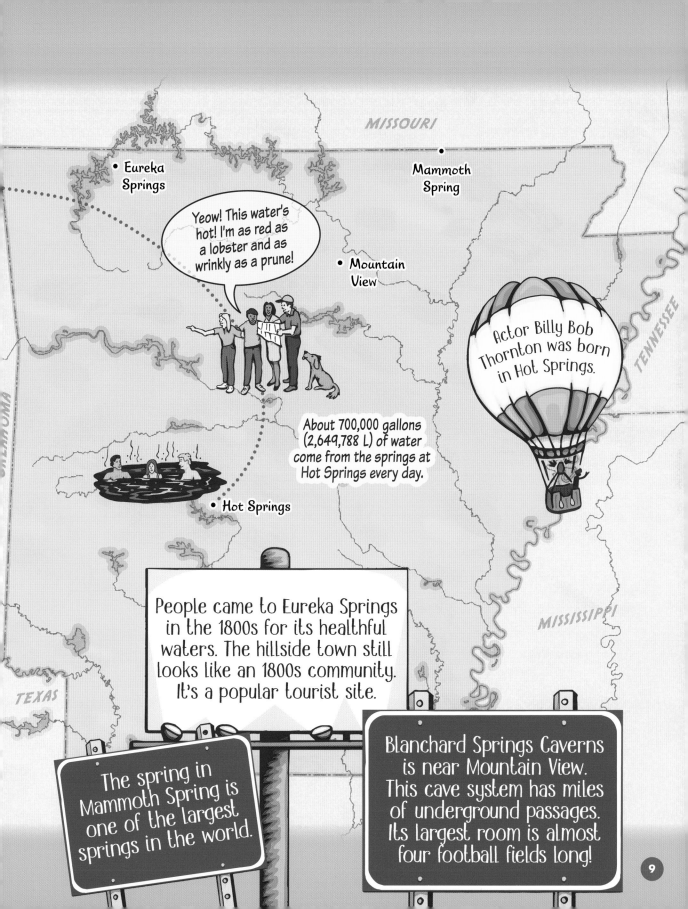

MISSOURI

• Eureka
  Springs

Mammoth
Spring

Yeow! This water's hot! I'm as red as a lobster and as wrinkly as a prune!

• Mountain
  View

Actor Billy Bob Thornton was born in Hot Springs.

About 700,000 gallons (2,649,788 L) of water come from the springs at Hot Springs every day.

• Hot Springs

OKLAHOMA

TENNESSEE

MISSISSIPPI

People came to Eureka Springs in the 1800s for its healthful waters. The hillside town still looks like an 1800s community. It's a popular tourist site.

TEXAS

The spring in Mammoth Spring is one of the largest springs in the world.

Blanchard Springs Caverns is near Mountain View. This cave system has miles of underground passages. Its largest room is almost four football fields long!

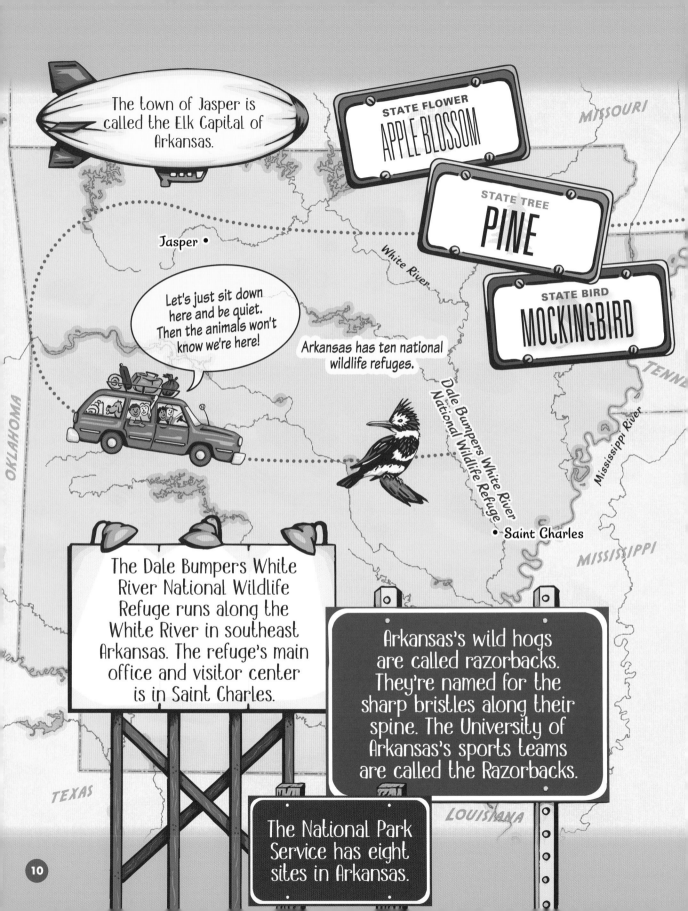

The town of Jasper is called the Elk Capital of Arkansas.

STATE FLOWER
APPLE BLOSSOM

STATE TREE
PINE

STATE BIRD
MOCKINGBIRD

Jasper •

Let's just sit down here and be quiet. Then the animals won't know we're here!

Arkansas has ten national wildlife refuges.

White River

Dale Bumpers White River National Wildlife Refuge

Mississippi River

• Saint Charles

The Dale Bumpers White River National Wildlife Refuge runs along the White River in southeast Arkansas. The refuge's main office and visitor center is in Saint Charles.

Arkansas's wild hogs are called razorbacks. They're named for the sharp bristles along their spine. The University of Arkansas's sports teams are called the Razorbacks.

The National Park Service has eight sites in Arkansas.

OKLAHOMA

MISSOURI

TENNE[SSEE]

MISSISSIPPI

TEXAS

LOUISIANA

EXPLORING WHITE RIVER NATIONAL WILDLIFE REFUGE

Creep through the Dale Bumpers White River National Wildlife Refuge. You're bound to see lots of animals. When's the best time to look for them? In the early morning or late afternoon. Animals roam around when the sun's not too hot.

Look by the river or around a pond. Animals go there to drink. You'll see deer, beavers, foxes, and wild hogs. You might even spot alligators or bears. You'll see plenty of turtles, lizards, and frogs. Kingfishers fish by the water, and ducks swim past you. Eagles and hawks soar high above you. They're looking for small animals to eat!

A variety of amphibians can be found at the Wildlife Refuge.

TOAD SUCK DAZE IN CONWAY

Pick out a toad from the toad pen. Or bring your own toad if you like. Then line up for the Toad Races. It's time for Toad Suck Daze!

This is a fun festival in Conway. It offers pet shows and music. There's a Baby Crawl race. And there's the Tour de Toad bike race. Don't miss the pancake breakfast!

No frogs may enter—only toads. What's the difference? Toads have rough, dry, bumpy skin. But frogs have smooth, moist skin. Happy hopping!

Grab a toad and head for the race in Conway!

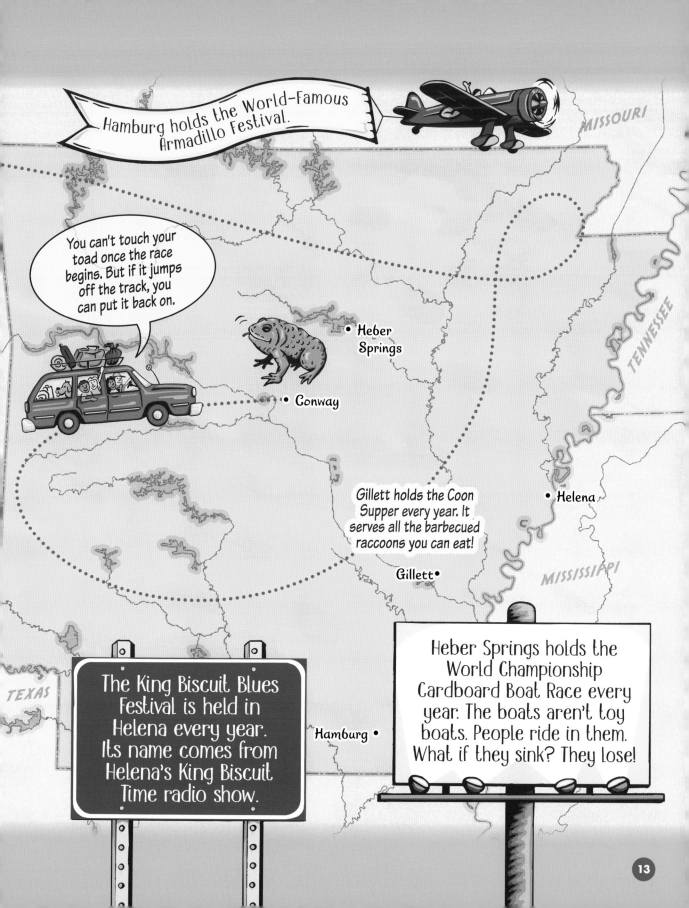

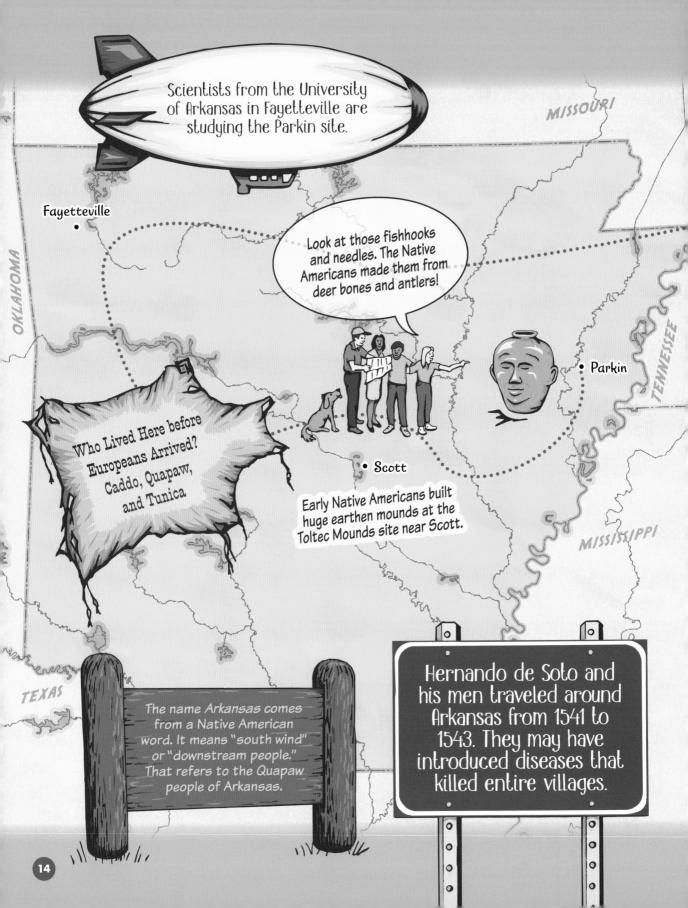

THE PARKIN ARCHEOLOGICAL* STATE PARK

Who lived in Arkansas 1,000 years ago? Just visit Parkin, and you'll see. A Native American community lived there from about 1000 to 1600 AD. A deep ditch surrounded their village for safety. They made pottery jugs molded to look like human faces. They grew corn, beans, and other crops.

Hernando de Soto arrived in Arkansas in 1541. He was a Spanish explorer. De Soto visited a village he called Casqui. **Historians** believe the Parkin site is that village. They think the village never had more than 2,000 people.

You can visit Parkin Archeological State Park. You'll see the Native Americans' art, pottery, and tools. And you'll watch **archaeologists** dig for ancient objects.

Archeological is the preferred spelling of the Parkin Archeological State Park.

Parkin has Native American artifacts that are over 1,000 years old.

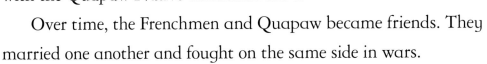

Want to walk through 300 years of history? Just stroll through Arkansas Post. It was Arkansas's first European settlement. Frenchman Henri de Tonti founded it in 1686. He started trading goods with the Quapaw Native American tribe.

Over time, the Frenchmen and Quapaw became friends. They married one another and fought on the same side in wars.

The United States took over present-day Arkansas in 1803 and the Quapaw were eventually forced onto reservations. Arkansas Territory was established in 1819. By then, Arkansas Post was a busy river port. It became the new territory's capital.

Arkansas Post was destroyed during the U.S. Civil War (1861–1865). Northern and Southern states were fighting over states's rights and slavery. Arkansas was on the Confederate side. Northern states formed the Union side. In the end, the Union won the war.

Arkansas Post was the first European settlement in Arkansas. Visit this state park to learn about its history!

The Quapaw village of Osotouy stood where Henri de Tonti set up Arkansas Post.

The Union won the Battle of Pea Ridge. It took place March 7–8, 1862.

Pea Ridge

MISSOURI

TENNESSEE

There's so much to do at Arkansas Post! We can take walks along trails, see exhibits, and watch movies.

Prairie Grove

The Battle of Prairie Grove was on December 7, 1862. It ended with a Union victory.

Mississippi River valley

The Battle of Arkansas Post took place January 9-11, 1863. More than 30,000 Union troops defeated 5,000 Confederate soldiers there.

Gillett

MISSISSIPPI

At Arkansas Post, you'll tour a pioneer home. You'll also see Quapaw pottery and old military equipment.

Arkansas was the 25th state to enter the Union. It joined on June 15, 1836.

René-Robert Cavelier, Sieur de La Salle, claimed the Mississippi River valley for France in 1682. That included present-day Arkansas.

Arkansas Post was the capital of Arkansas Territory from 1819 to 1821.

The Arkansas State Fiddler's Championship is held at Ozark Folk Center in Mountain View.

• Fayetteville

• Hogeye

Snowball •

Mountain View •

Actor Mary Steenburgen was born in Newport.

• Newport

• Fort Smith

In 2016, 2,988,248 people lived in Arkansas. It's the 33rd-largest state by population.

OKLAHOMA

TENNESSEE

• Greasy Corner

Watch that wood-carver! He's carving an old man's face onto that walking stick!

★ Little Rock

MISSISSIPPI

Country music singer Johnny Cash was born in Kingsland.

• Kingsland

You'll see people working at more than 20 crafts in the Ozark Folk Center's craft village.

Folk singer and songwriter Jimmy Driftwood was born near Mountain View.

Population of Largest Cities

Little Rock.....................197,992
Fort Smith.....................88,194
Fayetteville....................82,830

Arkansas has towns named Hogeye, Greasy Corner, and Snowball!

PIONEER LIFE IN MOUNTAIN VIEW

Suppose you lived way up in the mountains. How would you get soap, toys, or clothes? You'd make them!

That's what Arkansas **pioneers** did in the 1800s. They settled in the rugged mountains. They were far from towns or stores. Their skills helped them stay alive.

Mountain View preserves this way of life. Just visit the Ozark Folk Center State Park. You'll see people making brooms, pottery, and soap. Some are making dolls, candles, or musical instruments. Fiddlers and banjo players strike up tunes. And everyone's happy to explain what they're doing.

Children will learn what pioneer life was really like at the Ozark Folk Center!

LAW AND ORDER IN FORT SMITH

Glance around the old courtroom. You can almost hear the judge's booming voice. Look at the old jail cells. Many outlaws spent their last days here.

You're touring the Fort Smith National Historic Site. Judge Isaac Parker ruled over the court here. He was known for his harsh sentences.

Fort Smith is right on the Oklahoma border. In the 1800s, Oklahoma was Indian Territory before the U.S. government forced Native Americans onto reservations. Outlaws also roamed this land. But some got caught. Judge Parker's job was to decide their fate.

Many outlaws received their sentences from Judge Isaac Parker at the Fort Smith Courthouse.

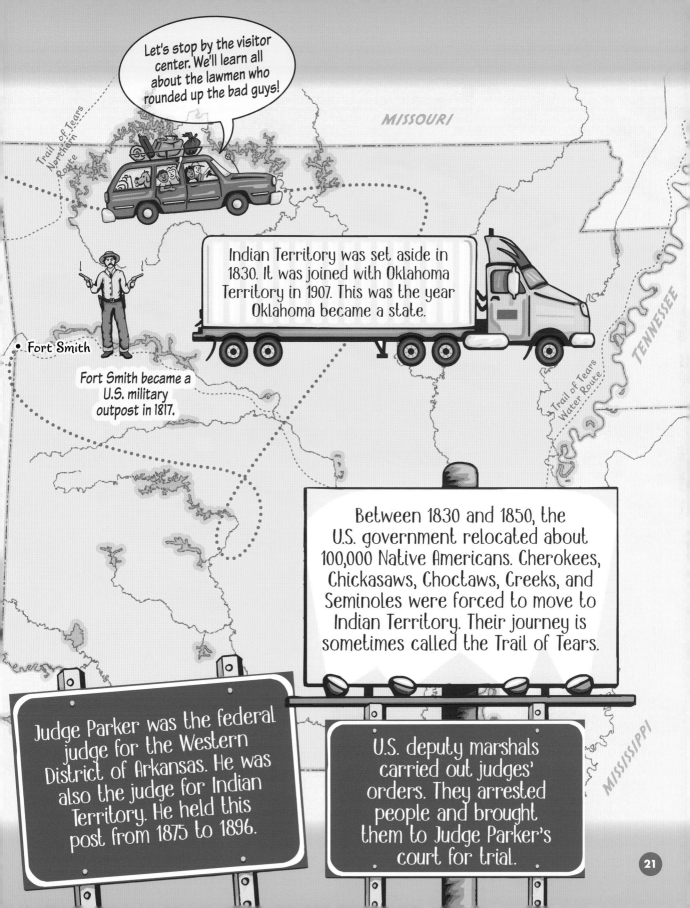

Let's stop by the visitor center. We'll learn all about the lawmen who rounded up the bad guys!

MISSOURI

Indian Territory was set aside in 1830. It was joined with Oklahoma Territory in 1907. This was the year Oklahoma became a state.

TENNESSEE

• Fort Smith

Fort Smith became a U.S. military outpost in 1817.

Trail of Tears Water Route

Between 1830 and 1850, the U.S. government relocated about 100,000 Native Americans. Cherokees, Chickasaws, Choctaws, Creeks, and Seminoles were forced to move to Indian Territory. Their journey is sometimes called the Trail of Tears.

Judge Parker was the federal judge for the Western District of Arkansas. He was also the judge for Indian Territory. He held this post from 1875 to 1896.

U.S. deputy marshals carried out judges' orders. They arrested people and brought them to Judge Parker's court for trial.

MISSISSIPPI

21

SMACKOVER'S MUSEUM OF NATURAL RESOURCES

Today, it's easy to get gasoline for cars. We just drive to a gas station. But things were different in the 1920s. Cars were a fairly new invention. And the oil **industry** was new, too. (Petroleum, or oil, is made into gasoline.)

You'll learn about these days in Smackover. Just visit the Arkansas Museum of Natural Resources! Outdoors, you'll see working oil **derricks**. Indoors, you'll see old cars and gas-station pumps.

Oil was discovered in El Dorado in 1921. Smackover's first oil well opened in 1922. Thousands of people swarmed in to get jobs. It was an exciting time!

This old crooked ladder is attached to a metal oil derrick.

WALMART'S BIRTHPLACE IN BENTONVILLE

Have you ever been to Walmart? These stores are named after Sam Walton. In 1950, he opened a little store in Bentonville. Now there are Walmart stores all over the world!

You can visit Walton's first Bentonville store. It's called the Walmart Museum now. It's a museum of Walmart history. You'll see Sam's old office and pickup truck. And you'll see some Ol' Roy Dog Food. It was named after Walton's dog!

Stores such as Walmart are busy in Arkansas. So are factories. Food products are the state's major factory goods. Many factories make paper and metal goods, too.

You can still visit Sam Walton's first store in Bentonville!

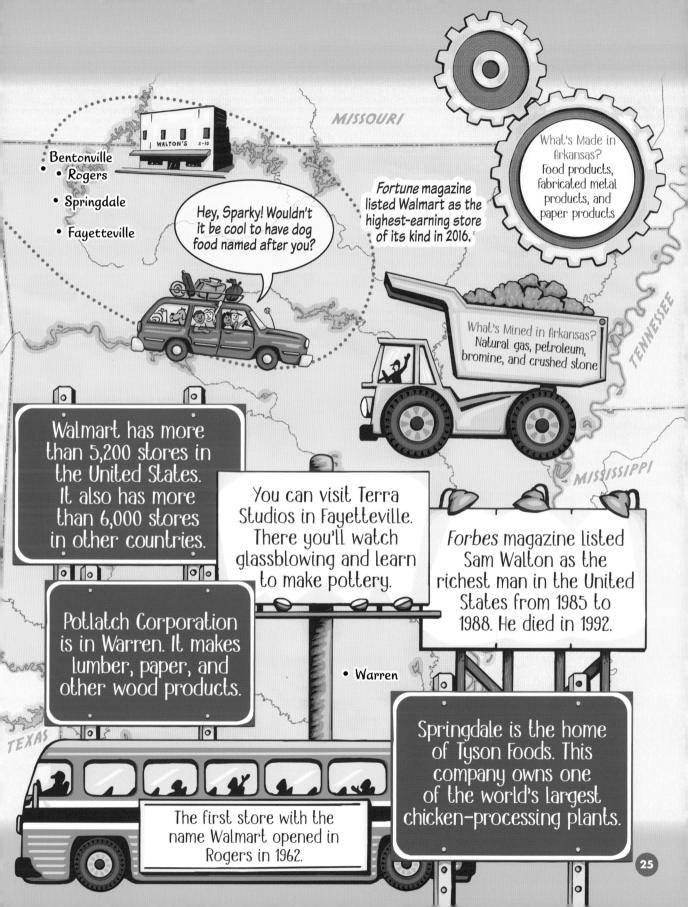

MISSOURI

WALTON'S 5-10

Bentonville
Rogers
Springdale
Fayetteville

Hey, Sparky! Wouldn't it be cool to have dog food named after you?

Fortune magazine listed Walmart as the highest-earning store of its kind in 2016.

What's Made in Arkansas? Food products, fabricated metal products, and paper products

What's Mined in Arkansas? Natural gas, petroleum, bromine, and crushed stone

TENNESSEE

MISSISSIPPI

Walmart has more than 5,200 stores in the United States. It also has more than 6,000 stores in other countries.

You can visit Terra Studios in Fayetteville. There you'll watch glassblowing and learn to make pottery.

Forbes magazine listed Sam Walton as the richest man in the United States from 1985 to 1988. He died in 1992.

Potlatch Corporation is in Warren. It makes lumber, paper, and other wood products.

Warren

TEXAS

The first store with the name Walmart opened in Rogers in 1962.

Springdale is the home of Tyson Foods. This company owns one of the world's largest chicken-processing plants.

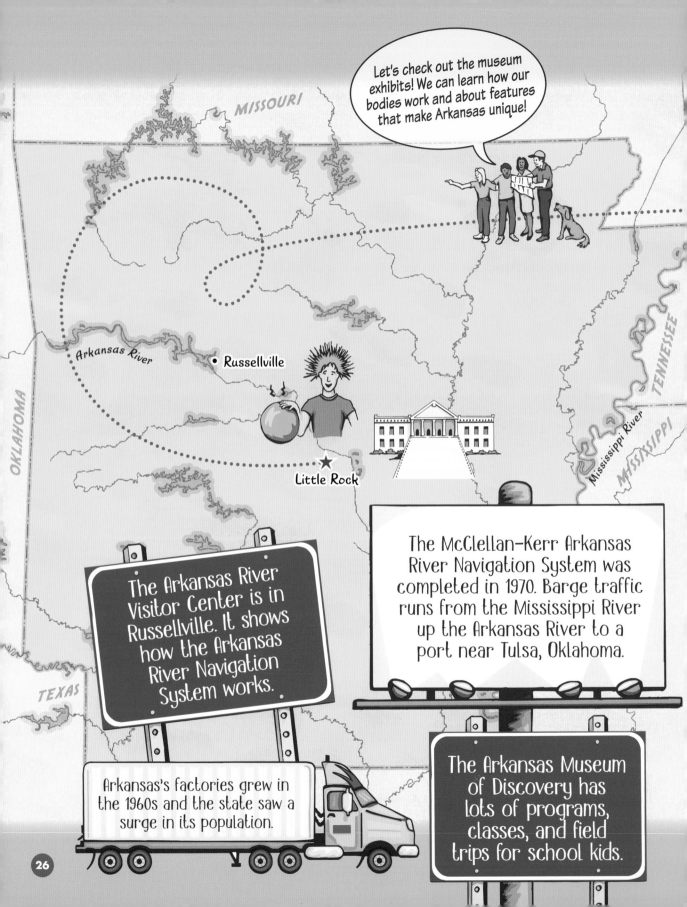

Let's check out the museum exhibits! We can learn how our bodies work and about features that make Arkansas unique!

MISSOURI

OKLAHOMA

Arkansas River

• Russellville

Little Rock

TEXAS

TENNESSEE

Mississippi River

MISSISSIPPI

The Arkansas River Visitor Center is in Russellville. It shows how the Arkansas River Navigation System works.

The McClellan-Kerr Arkansas River Navigation System was completed in 1970. Barge traffic runs from the Mississippi River up the Arkansas River to a port near Tulsa, Oklahoma.

Arkansas's factories grew in the 1960s and the state saw a surge in its population.

The Arkansas Museum of Discovery has lots of programs, classes, and field trips for school kids.

LITTLE ROCK'S ARKANSAS MUSEUM OF DISCOVERY

Use your body's energy to turn lights on. Feel electricity make your hair stand straight out. Meet creepy, crawly bugs and even hold some. See what the dentist sees inside your mouth. You're exploring the Arkansas Museum of Discovery in Little Rock!

Scientific discoveries helped Arkansas grow. Scientists and engineers developed better farm equipment. Farms then needed fewer workers. People moved to cities for factory work.

Waterway engineers improved the Arkansas River, too. Then large chains of **barges** could use the river. This brought new business to Arkansas's river ports. Look for barges when you cross the Arkansas River!

There are many things to learn at the Museum of Discovery!

THE STATE CAPITOL IN LITTLE ROCK

Does the Little Rock capitol building look familiar to you? It should. It looks like the U.S. Capitol in Washington, DC. That's where the nation's lawmakers meet. Sometimes moviemakers want to show the U.S. Capitol. They film the Arkansas capitol instead!

Many state government offices are in the capitol. Arkansas's state government has three branches. One branch makes the laws. Its members belong to the General Assembly. They meet in the capitol. A second branch carries out the laws. It's headed by the governor. Judges make up the third branch of government. They decide whether someone has broken the law.

The capitol building took 16 years to build.

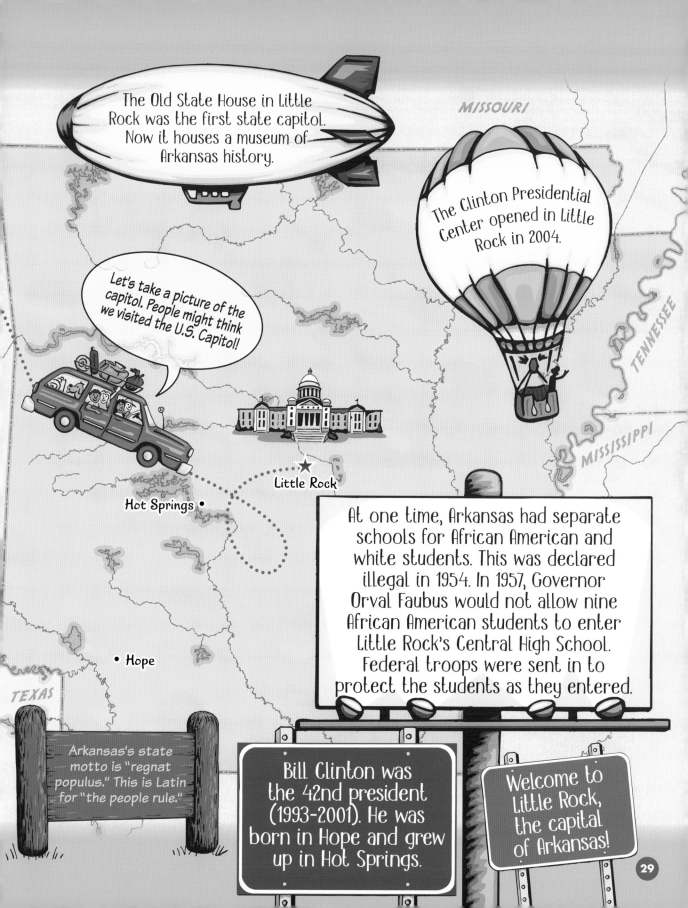

The Old State House in Little Rock was the first state capitol. Now it houses a museum of Arkansas history.

The Clinton Presidential Center opened in Little Rock in 2004.

MISSOURI

TENNESSEE

MISSISSIPPI

Let's take a picture of the capitol. People might think we visited the U.S. Capitol!

★
Little Rock

Hot Springs •

• Hope

TEXAS

At one time, Arkansas had separate schools for African American and white students. This was declared illegal in 1954. In 1957, Governor Orval Faubus would not allow nine African American students to enter Little Rock's Central High School. Federal troops were sent in to protect the students as they entered.

Arkansas's state motto is "regnat populus." This is Latin for "the people rule."

Bill Clinton was the 42nd president (1993-2001). He was born in Hope and grew up in Hot Springs.

Welcome to Little Rock, the capital of Arkansas!

Stuttgart is home to the Museum of the Arkansas Grand Prairie. It shows how Arkansas became the nation's top rice producer.

They've got turtle races at the tomato festival. Turtles love tomatoes. They have to be fast to get the juiciest ones!

• Tontitown

• Lincoln

Mountain View •

Weiner •

Altus •
• Clarksville

The state fair is held in Little Rock in early autumn each year.

★ Little Rock

Warren is in Bradley County. Farmers there grow pink tomatoes: Bradleys and Arkansas Travelers. Look for them in farmers' markets.

Stuttgart •

Some Arkansas Farm Product Festivals
Apple Festival (Lincoln)
Bean Festival (Mountain View)
Grape Festival (Tontitown)
Peach Festival (Clarksville)
Rice Festival (Weiner)
Watermelon Festival (Hope)
Wine Festival (Altus)

• Hope

Warren •

OKLAHOMA

TENNESSEE

MISSISSIPPI

TEXAS

LOUISIANA

What Does Arkansas Raise? Broilers (chickens), beef cattle, cotton, and rice

The pink tomato is Arkansas's official state fruit and vegetable. Tomatoes are actually fruits. But people use them as vegetables.

WARREN'S PINK TOMATO FESTIVAL

Do you like tomatoes? Then try the tomato-eating contest. Do you have a dog? You might want to enter it in the cutest dog contest. Are you still hungry? Then belly up to the all-tomato lunch. You're at the Pink Tomato Festival in Warren!

Tomatoes are a delicious Arkansas product. But rice and soybeans are the leading crops. No other state grows more rice. Arkansas is a top chicken state, too. Chickens bring in the most farm income. Many farmers raise beef cattle, hogs, and turkeys. Wild turkeys live in the woods. Want a turkey to come running? Then practice your turkey calls. Turkey calling is a fine art in Arkansas!

Arkansas takes pride in its pink tomatoes.

DIGGING FOR DIAMONDS IN MURFREESBORO

Bring your bucket and shovel. Then start digging for diamonds. What if you find one? Finders keepers!

You're diamond hunting at the Crater of Diamonds State Park in Murfreesboro. It's the nation's only diamond-mining site. Thousands of diamonds have been found there. Most are tiny, but some are huge.

Diamonds aren't sparkly when you dig them up. They're sort of dark and greasy looking. How can you tell a diamond from gravel? Park workers help you. They teach you what raw diamonds look like. And they show you how to search. Good luck!

Come dig for diamonds in Arkansas!

Oh, boy! An average of two diamonds are found here every day. Let's find them!

Arkansas diamonds are harder than the average diamond.

More than 75,000 diamonds have been found at the Crater of Diamonds.

• Murfreesboro

The Uncle Sam was the biggest diamond ever found at the Crater of Diamonds. It was discovered in 1924. Uncle Sam weighed more than 40 carats.

Diamonds are measured by weight. The carat is the standard of weight for gold and jewels. There are about 142 carats in 1 ounce.

You might also find garnets, amethysts, jasper, agates, and quartz at the Crater of Diamonds.

MISSOURI

MISSISSIPPI

TEXAS

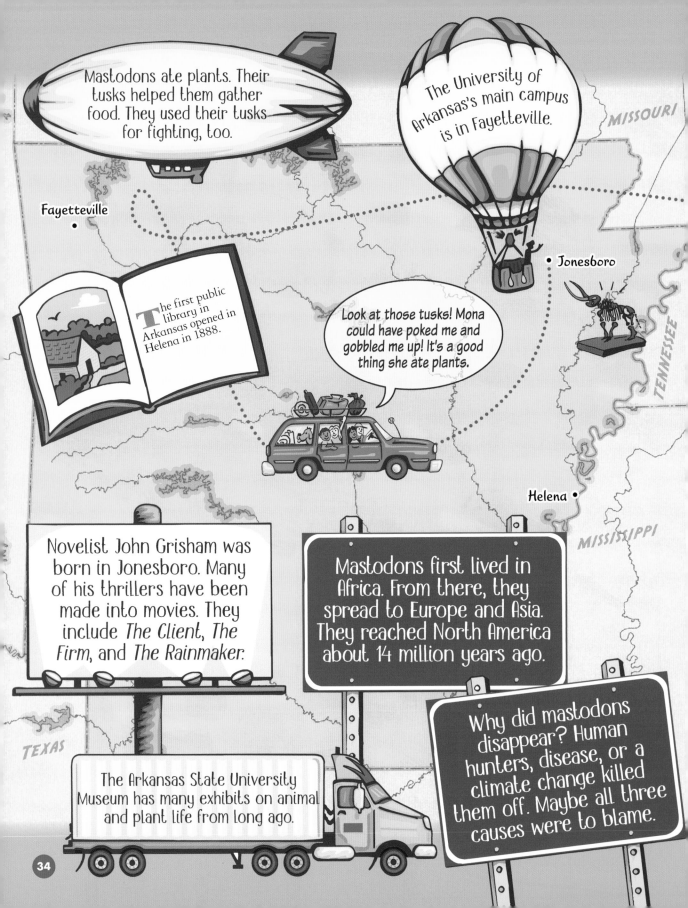

MEET MONA THE MASTODON

Watch out! She's pretty tall. In fact, you barely come up to her knees. She's Mona the mastodon!

Mastodons are relatives of elephants. They lived millions of years ago. They had shaggy coats and long, curved tusks. Mona is a copy of a real mastodon skeleton. You'll find her in Jonesboro. She's in the Arkansas State University Museum.

Arkansas was a great place for mastodons. They've been found in 20 sites there. Mastodons disappeared about 10,000 years ago. Now, take a long look at Mona.

Are you glad or sad that mastodons are gone?

Mastodons lived millions of years ago and once called Arkansas home.

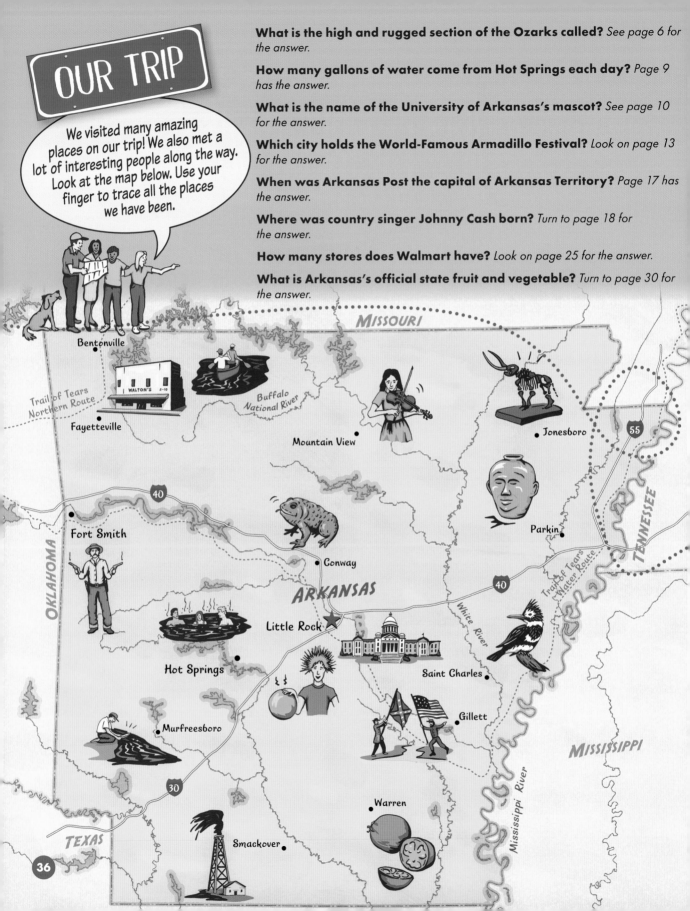

OUR TRIP

We visited many amazing places on our trip! We also met a lot of interesting people along the way. Look at the map below. Use your finger to trace all the places we have been.

What is the high and rugged section of the Ozarks called? *See page 6 for the answer.*

How many gallons of water come from Hot Springs each day? *Page 9 has the answer.*

What is the name of the University of Arkansas's mascot? *See page 10 for the answer.*

Which city holds the World-Famous Armadillo Festival? *Look on page 13 for the answer.*

When was Arkansas Post the capital of Arkansas Territory? *Page 17 has the answer.*

Where was country singer Johnny Cash born? *Turn to page 18 for the answer.*

How many stores does Walmart have? *Look on page 25 for the answer.*

What is Arkansas's official state fruit and vegetable? *Turn to page 30 for the answer.*

MISSOURI

Bentonville

Trail of Tears
Northern Route

Fayetteville

WALTON'S 5-10

Buffalo
National River

Mountain View

Jonesboro

55

OKLAHOMA

Fort Smith

Conway

ARKANSAS

Little Rock

Hot Springs

Saint Charles

Murfreesboro

Gillett

Parkin

White River

Trail of Tears
Water Route

TENNESSEE

40

40

30

Warren

Smackover

TEXAS

Mississippi River

MISSISSIPPI

STATE SYMBOLS

State beverage: Milk

State bird: Mockingbird

State flower: Apple blossom

State folk dance: Square dance

State fruit and vegetable:
Vine ripe pink tomato

State gem: Diamond

State insect: Honeybee

State mammal: White-tailed deer

State mineral: Quartz crystal

State musical instrument: Fiddle

State rock: Bauxite

State tree: Pine

STATE SONG

"ARKANSAS"

Arkansas has two official state songs. They are "Arkansas (You Run Deep in Me)" by Wayland Holyfield and "Oh, Arkansas" by Terry Rose and Gary Klaff. Arkansas also has an official state historical song, "The Arkansas Traveler." The official state anthem is "Arkansas" by Eva Ware Barnett. Words and music by Eva Ware Barnett

I am thinking tonight of the
  Southland,
Of the home of my childhood
  days,
Where I roamed through the
  woods and the meadows
By the mill and the brook that
  plays;
Where the roses are in bloom
And the sweet magnolia, too,
Where the jasmine is white
And the fields are violet blue,
There a welcome awaits all her
  children
Who have wandered afar from
  home.

Chorus:
Arkansas, Arkansas, 'tis a name
  dear,
'Tis the place I call "home, sweet
  home";

Arkansas, Arkansas, I salute thee,
From thy shelter no more I'll
  roam.

'Tis a land full of joy and of
  sunshine,
Rich in pearls and in diamonds
  rare,
Full of hope, faith, and love for
  the stranger,
Who may pass 'neath her portals
  fair;
There the rice fields are full,
And the cotton, corn, and hay,
There the fruits of the field,
Bloom in the winter months and
  May,
'Tis the land that I love, first of all,
  dear,
And to her let us all give cheer.

(Chorus)

That was a great trip! We have traveled all over Arkansas. There are a few places that we didn't have time for, though. Next time, we plan to visit the Arkansas Alligator Farm and Petting Zoo in Hot Springs. They have over 300 alligators. Some are up to 10 feet (3.0m) long! Visitors can also see deer, goats, wolves, and peacocks.

FAMOUS PEOPLE

Angelou, Maya (1928–2014), author and poet

Bates, Daisy Lee Gatson (1914–1999), civil rights activist

Campbell, Glen (1936–), singer, guitarist, and songwriter

Cash, Johnny (1932–2003), singer and songwriter

Cleaver, Eldridge (1935–1998), civil rights activist and author

Clinton, Bill (1946–), 42nd U.S. president

Fletcher, John Gould (1886–1950), poet

Fulbright, J. William (1905–1995), politician and educator

Green, David Gordon (1975–), film director

Grisham, John (1955–), novelist

Huckabee, Mike (1955–), former governor of Arkansas

Jones, E. Fay (1921–2004), architect and designer

Joplin, Scott (1868–1917), composer and pianist

Ladd, Alan (1913–1964), actor

Liston, Sonny (1932–1970), professional boxer

MacArthur, Douglas (1880–1964), World War II general

Martin, Mark (1959–), NASCAR driver

Pippen, Scottie (1965–), basketball player

Saracen (ca. 1735–1832), Quapaw American Native chief

Stone, Edward Durell (1902–1978), architect

Thornton, Billy Bob (1955–), actor

Walton, Sam (1918–1992), founder of Walmart

Wood, Audrey (1930–), children's book author and illustrator

WORDS TO KNOW

archaeologists (ar-kee-oh-LOJ-ists) people who study human history by looking at artifacts and physical remains

barges (BAR-jez) long boats with flat bottoms

bathhouse (BATH-houss) a building where people take healthful baths

derricks (DER-iks) towers with equipment for drilling into the ground for oil

historians (hi-STOR-ree-unz) people who study events in history

industry (IN-duh-stree) a type of business

pioneers (pye-uh-NEERZ) people who settle in a new area

State flag

State seal

TO LEARN MORE

IN THE LIBRARY

Marsh, Carole. *I'm Reading about Arkansas*. Peachtree City, GA: Gallopade International, 2014.

Oachs, Emily Rose. *Arkansas: The Natural State*. Minneapolis, MN: Bellwether, 2014.

O'Brien, Cynthia. *Explore with Sieur de la Salle*. New York, NY: Crabtree, 2015.

Stuckey, Rachel. *Explore with Hernando de Soto*. New York, NY: Crabtree, 2017.

Zabludoff, Marc. *Mastodon*. Tarrytown, NY: Marshall Cavendish Benchmark, 2011.

ON THE WEB

Visit our Web site for links about Arkansas:
childsworld.com/links

Note to Parents, Teachers, and Librarians: We routinely verify our Web links to make sure they are safe and active sites. So encourage your readers to check them out!

PLACES TO VISIT OR CONTACT

Arkansas Department of Parks and Tourism
arkansas.com
One Capitol Mall
Little Rock, AR 72201
501/682-7777
For more information about traveling in Arkansas

Arkansas History Commission
ark-ives.com
One Capitol Mall
Little Rock, AR 72201
501/682-6900
For more information about the history of Arkansas

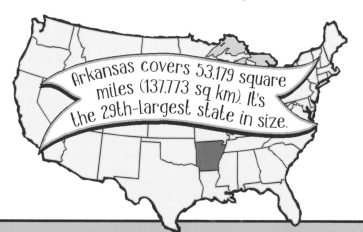

Arkansas covers 53,179 square miles (137,773 sq km). It's the 29th-largest state in size.

INDEX

Bye, Land of Opportunity. We had a great time. We'll come back soon!